How a Law is Born

By
Dr. Latina Campbell

Print ISBN: 978-1-966491-08-8

eBook ISBN: 978-1-966491-09-5

Printed in the United States of America

Story Corner Publishing & Consulting, Inc.

Chesapeake, VA 23321

Storycornerpublishing@yahoo.com

www.StoryCornerPublishing.com

Dedication

I dedicate this book to all the children who dream of becoming the future president, members of Congress, judges, lawyers, politicians, law enforcement, or even military. Be fair and just with everyone and do everything in love and kindness. Put God first and allow Him to lead you through every decision.

In the meantime, remember no matter who holds office or what laws are passed, God has the final say and remains in control. There's no need to worry about things you see happen in the world, just pray to God. Prayer changes everything.

P.S.

I'm proud of you because you are brave!

Have you ever wondered, "Where do laws come from?

Do they grow on trees or under the sun?"

Nope! They start as an idea in someone's mind,

Then take a long journey of a special kind.

It all begins with a question or need,

Like, "How can we help people succeed?"

Someone might say, "Let's make a new rule!"

And that's how a law starts—it's pretty cool!

This idea becomes a bill, which is kind of a draft,

A written-down plan of the law they've graphed.

The bill is introduced in Congress, you see,

That's the House and Senate—it's step number three!

First, the bill goes to a special committee,

A group of lawmakers, both sharp and witty.

They read the bill and talk it through,

"Is it helpful? Is it fair? What will it do?"

9

The committee votes to send it ahead,

Or they might say, "This bill is dead."

If the bill moves on, it's time for debate,

In the House or Senate, it's quite the fate!

In the House of Representatives, the members discuss,

They argue, they question—they're thinking of us!

If most members vote "yes," it goes to the Senate,

Where more lawmakers will then examine it.

13

The Senate talks and makes their case,

They read and discuss it all over the place.

If they agree and the vote says "yes,"

The bill's one step closer to lawfulness!

15

But wait! There's one more big, important stop,

The President's desk—it's the very top.

The President looks at the bill and decides,

"Should this be a law for the nationwide?"

If the President says, "Yes, I agree,"

The bill becomes a law for you and me!

But if the President says, "No, not now,"

That's called a veto, and here's how:

The bill goes back to Congress once more,

Where lawmakers can try to settle the score.

If enough members vote to override,

The bill becomes a law—it can't be denied!

It takes teamwork, time, and a lot of debate,

To pass a law that's fair and great.

It's a process to make sure the rules we need,

Help everyone, no matter their creed.

So next time you hear of a brand-new law,

You'll know how it happened—step by step, with no flaw.

It all starts with an idea that's shared,

And a journey to show how much we cared.

25

From bill to law, it's a long, hard climb,

But worth it to make our world sublime.

Laws keep us safe and make things right,

For every person, day and night.

The End

www.ingramcontent.com/pod-product-compliance
Lightning Source LLC
Chambersburg PA
CBHW080128150626
46550CB00017B/2830